MW00941612

JONATHAN SALGADO

HOW TO START A CLOTHING BRAND FROM SCRATCH

HOW TO BUILD A CLOTHING BRAND FROM SCRATCH:
THE ULTIMATE STEP-BY-STEP GUIDE TO CREATING
YOUR CLOTHING BRAND

First Edition, October 2024
© 2024, Jonathan Salgado
All rights reserved.

ISBN: 9798341313613

*For the entrepreneurs who push boundaries and
for those who educate, influence, and inspire
others to make their dreams a reality.*

Introduction

Fashion is not limited to clothing; it is a form of self-expression, a showcase of identity, and for many, a dream come true. However, creating a clothing brand from an idea can be a challenging and uncertain journey. In this book, I want to share with you my personal experience on this path, as well as the lessons learned and the methods that helped me build a brand from scratch.

My Personal Experience in Creating a Clothing Brand:
From conceptualizing the brand's vision to manufacturing the garments, I faced numerous challenges during my own brand creation process. There were moments of uncertainty and disorientation, but also of learning and progress. Throughout this journey, I learned the importance of having a structured approach and a clear guide. This led me to write this book with the aim of helping other entrepreneurs avoid making the same mistakes I did and finding their own path to success.

Purpose:
This book is intended to serve as a step-by-step guide for anyone interested in establishing their own clothing brand, regardless of their level of experience. Here, you will find useful information to help you navigate each stage of the process, from those who are just starting to those who already have a clearer idea of what they want. Making clothes is not everything; it's about building a brand that inspires and connects with people.

Who Is This Book For?
This book is for you if you have ever dreamed of creating your own clothing line, if you feel you have a unique idea that you must share with the world, or if you simply want to learn more about the fashion industry. It is aimed at entrepreneurs with little or no experience in the sector and those looking to give new momentum to their existing projects. Throughout the following pages, I will provide helpful tips, useful tools, and real-life examples that will help you turn your vision into a successful brand.

A Journey of Transformation:
I invite you to experiment, try out, and adjust your approach as needed as you progress through the reading. Creating a clothing brand is not a linear path, and it is crucial to be open to innovation and adaptability. You can achieve your goals with patience and perseverance and create a brand that not only represents you but also resonates with your audience.

1. Defining Your Brand's Vision and Mission

Creating a successful clothing brand begins with a solid foundation, which is your vision and mission. These components will guide every decision you make and help you effectively communicate what your brand represents. This chapter will explain why it is crucial to have a clear vision, how to define your brand's values and purpose, and what strategies can help you differentiate yourself from others in a competitive market.

Why Is It Important to Have a Clear Vision?
A clear vision is the beacon that guides your brand. Here's why it is fundamental:
- **Direction and Focus:** Having a well-defined vision provides a sense of direction. It helps you set short- and long-term goals, allowing you to focus your efforts on what truly matters for your brand.
- **Motivation and Commitment:** An inspiring vision not only motivates the founders but also attracts collaborators, partners, and employees. When everyone shares the same vision, a sense of belonging and commitment to the brand's success is generated.
- **Effective Communication:** A clear vision facilitates communicating your brand's identity to your audience. It helps build an emotional connection with customers, who will feel drawn to your values and purposes.

Defining Your Brand's Values and Purpose
Values and purpose are at the core of your brand. To define them, consider the following steps:
- **Identify Your Values:**
1. Make a list of principles that are important to you and that you want your brand to represent. This may include sustainability, inclusivity, authenticity, quality, among others.
2. Reflect on personal or professional experiences that have influenced your values and how these can be integrated into your brand.
- **Define Your Purpose:**
3. Ask yourself: What problem does your brand seek to solve? How do you want to impact your customers and society?
4. A clear purpose can be the motivation behind your business decisions and can differentiate you from the competition.
- **Draft Your Mission Statement:** Combine your values and purpose into a concise mission statement. This statement should communicate who you are, what you do, and why you do it. For example: "Our mission is to create sustainable fashion that empowers people to express themselves authentically while caring for the planet."

How to Differentiate Yourself in a Competitive Market

In the fashion world, competition is fierce. To stand out, consider the following strategies:

- **Find Your Niche:** Identify a market segment that is underserved or that could benefit from your unique approach. This could be based on style, target audience, or sustainability, for example.
- **Create a Unique Value Proposition (UVP):** Your value proposition should communicate what makes you different from the competition. It could be the quality of your materials, the exclusivity of your designs, or a genuine commitment to ethical practices.
- **Build a Strong Brand Identity:** Your visual identity (logo, color palette, typography) and brand voice should be consistent and reflect your values. A strong brand identity helps create recognition and loyalty among customers.
- **Effective Communication:** Use social media and other marketing platforms to communicate your vision, mission, and values. Transparency in your business practices is also key to building trust with your customers.
- **Foster a Community:** Create a connection with your customers beyond the transaction. Engage them in your brand's story through content, events, and collaborations. A loyal community can be your best ambassador.

Examples of Successful Brands

To inspire you, here are some examples of brands that have clearly defined their vision and mission:

- **Patagonia:** Their mission is "We're in business to save our home planet." Their focus on sustainability and ethics has resonated strongly with their audience.
- **TOMS:** Known for its "One for One" model, TOMS communicates its purpose of helping needy communities with every pair of shoes sold.

Practical Exercises

To help you define your brand's vision and mission, here are some practical exercises:

- **Values Exercise:** Write a list of 5 to 10 values that are important to you. Then, select the 3 that you consider most fundamental and note why they are significant for your brand.
- **Purpose in a Sentence:** Write a sentence that summarizes your brand's purpose. Ask yourself: What problem am I solving and how does this impact my customers?
- **Mission Statement:** Use the information gathered to draft a clear and concise mission statement that reflects your vision, values, and purpose.

Conclusion of Chapter 1

The first step in the process of creating a clothing brand is to establish the brand's vision and mission. Your values and purpose lay the foundation of your identity, while a clear vision provides direction and motivation. Finding a niche and developing a distinctive value proposition will allow you to stand out and attract customers who resonate with your brand in a competitive market. Remember that as you progress on this journey, your vision and mission may change and adapt, but always maintaining the essence of what you want to achieve.

2. Market Research and Competition Analysis

To create a clothing brand, it is essential to understand the environment in which you will operate. A comprehensive market study will help you find opportunities, understand your audience, and analyze your competitors. In this chapter, we will discuss how to find your market niche, the tools to research the competition, how to analyze trends in the fashion industry, and practical cases of brands that have established themselves in the market.

How to Identify Your Market Niche

Identifying your market niche is a crucial step to differentiate yourself in a saturated sector. Here are some steps to help you in this process:

- **Self-knowledge:** Reflect on your interests, skills, and values. What aspects of fashion are you passionate about? This will allow you to align your brand with what truly motivates you.
- **Audience research:** Identify who you want to target with your brand. Conduct surveys, interviews, and focus groups to better understand their needs, desires, and buying behaviors.
- **Competitor analysis:** Study your competitors. What niches are they occupying, and which ones seem to be underserved? Identifying gaps in the market will help you define a unique niche.
- **Market trends:** Research current trends in fashion. Is there a growing demand for sustainable, inclusive, or personalized products? Aligning your niche with market trends can increase your chances of success.
- **Unique Value Proposition (UVP):** Define what makes you different from others in the market. Your UVP should communicate how your brand will solve a specific problem for your audience.

Tools for Researching the Competition

Knowing your competitors will allow you to position yourself strategically in the market. Here are some tools you can use for effective research:

- **SWOT Analysis:** Conduct a SWOT analysis (Strengths, Weaknesses, Opportunities, Threats) of your competitors. This will help you understand their advantages and areas for improvement. Example: If a competitor has a strong presence on social media, that may be a strength you need to consider when developing your strategy.

- **Google and Social Media:** Use search tools like Google to research your competitors. Examine their websites, blogs, and social media profiles to understand their marketing and engagement strategies.

- **Web Analytics Tools:** Use tools like SimilarWeb or SEMrush to gather information about their website traffic, traffic sources, and the keywords they use. Tip: Look for high-volume, low-competition keywords that your competitors may be using.

- **Industry Reports:** Consult fashion industry reports that analyze trends and competitors. Platforms like Statista or Euromonitor can be valuable resources. Be sure to read trend reports specific to your niche.

- **Customer Feedback:** Read reviews and comments from customers about your competitors on platforms like Google, Facebook, and Instagram. This will give you insight into what customers value and what could be improved. Suggestion: Note common points in negative and positive reviews to identify opportunities for improvement.

Analyzing Trends in the Fashion Industry

Fashion trends can change rapidly, so it's crucial to stay updated. Here are some tips for effectively analyzing trends:

- **Fashion Publications and Blogs:** Follow well-known fashion magazines and blogs to keep abreast of the latest trends. Publications like Vogue, Business of Fashion, and WWD are reliable resources. Tip: Subscribe to newsletters to receive regular updates.
- **Social Media:** Platforms like Instagram, Pinterest, and TikTok are excellent for identifying emerging trends. Observe which styles, colors, and designs are gaining popularity. Use relevant hashtags to discover trend-related content.
- **Fashion Events:** Attend fashion fairs and events, both in-person and virtual, to observe trends firsthand. Events like Fashion Week and Première Vision are valuable opportunities for inspiration. Tip: Participate in webinars and panel discussions to learn from industry experts.
- **Data Analysis:** Use tools like Google Trends to analyze which search terms are on the rise. This can give you insights into consumer preferences. Suggestion: Compare trends over time to identify patterns.
- **Collaborations and Launches:** Keep an eye on brand collaborations and limited collection launches. These initiatives often set trends and can provide ideas about what is working in the market.

Practical Cases of Brands that Found Their Place in the Market

To illustrate how to identify a niche and establish a successful brand, here are some examples of brands that have managed to stand out:

- **Gymshark:** This sportswear brand focused on a specific niche: fitness and gym culture. Through effective social media marketing strategies and collaboration with influencers, Gymshark built a loyal community and became one of the most recognized brands in the sector.
- **Reformation:** With a focus on sustainability, Reformation has captured the attention of environmentally conscious consumers. Its commitment to ethical practices and transparency in production has resonated with its audience, allowing them to find a niche in eco-friendly fashion.
- **Alo Yoga:** Alo Yoga has established its place in the market by merging fashion with wellness. Its marketing strategy centers around lifestyle and self-care, which has enabled them to connect with an audience seeking not only quality clothing but also a holistic experience.

Practical Exercises

To help you apply what you've learned in this chapter, here are some practical exercises:

- **Niche Definition:** Write a list of your interests and skills in fashion. Then, research and note at least three market niches that interest you and are not saturated.
- **SWOT Analysis:** Conduct a SWOT analysis for at least three competitors in your niche. Identify their strengths, weaknesses, opportunities, and threats.
- **Fashion Trends:** Spend time researching current trends in fashion using at least three of the sources mentioned in this chapter. Note the trends that inspire you the most.
- **Case Study:** Select a fashion brand you admire and analyze its unique value proposition. What makes it different, and how has it positioned itself in the market?
- **Data Interpretation:** Gather data from your research and analyze how you can apply those insights to your strategy. What aspects of the competition should you imitate or avoid?

Conclusion of Chapter 2

The first steps to establishing a solid clothing brand are market research and competitive analysis. You will be able to make informed decisions that help you differentiate yourself by identifying your niche, using effective research tools, and analyzing industry trends. Success stories from brands can provide valuable lessons and inspire you on your own journey. Remember that adaptability and constant market observation are essential to maintaining relevance and success in the competitive world of fashion.

3. Naming Your Brand

One of the most significant components of your business identity is your brand name. It's the first impression consumers will have of you, and it should reflect the essence of your brand. In this chapter, we'll discuss how to choose a name that's appropriate for your brand, how to check its availability, and tips to ensure your name resonates with your audience.

How to Choose a Name that Represents Your Brand

Choosing the right name can be challenging, but with the right approach, you can find a name that encapsulates your brand's essence. Here are some steps you can follow:

- **Reflect on Your Vision and Mission:** Before you start brainstorming names, it's essential to be clear on what your brand represents. Review the vision and mission you defined in Chapter 1. Your name should align with these values and goals.
- **Identify Your Target Audience:** Think about who your ideal customers are. What kind of name will resonate with them? Consider their age, interests, and lifestyle. A name aimed at a younger audience might differ from one targeting a more mature crowd.
- **Brainstorm:** Have a brainstorming session and write down all the names that come to mind. Don't hold back; write down any word or phrase that inspires you. Use tools like online name generators for additional ideas. You can combine words, use synonyms, or explore different languages.
- **Simplicity and Memorability:** Look for names that are easy to pronounce and remember. A complicated name can be difficult for customers to share or keep in mind. Opt for short, catchy names that stick with your audience.
- **Avoid Trendy Words:** While it might be tempting to use trendy words, it's better to go for timeless names that won't become outdated quickly. This will ensure your brand remains relevant and enduring.
- **Test the Name Out Loud:** Once you have a shortlist of names, say each one out loud. Make sure it sounds good and doesn't have any negative or awkward connotations in other languages or cultures.

Common Mistakes When Choosing a Name

When picking a name for your brand, it's easy to fall into some common traps. Here are a few mistakes you should avoid:

- **Being Too Generic:** A generic name can cause your brand to get lost among the competition. Make sure your name has a unique twist that makes it stand out.
- **Ignoring Cultural Significance:** Before settling on a name, research its meaning across different cultures and languages. What might sound great in your native language could have negative connotations elsewhere.
- **Not Thinking About the Future:** Choose a name that can grow with you and doesn't limit your potential expansion into future product lines or markets.

Checking Name Availability

Once you've selected a few potential names, it's crucial to check their availability to avoid legal issues and confusion. Here are some steps to ensure your name is available:

- **Domain Name Registration:** Check if the web domain for your chosen name is available. You can use platforms like GoDaddy, Namecheap, or Google Domains to search. A .com domain is usually the best option as it's easier for people to remember.
- **Social Media Handles:** Make sure the name is available on popular social media platforms (Instagram, Facebook, Twitter, TikTok, etc.). Consistency across social media is essential for building your brand. Tools like Namecheckr or Knowem can help you check availability on multiple platforms simultaneously.
- **Trademark Registration:** Research whether the name is already registered as a trademark. You can do this through your country's trademark office (e.g., the Spanish Patent and Trademark Office in Spain or the USPTO in the U.S.). Registering your trademark will protect you legally and prevent future conflicts.
- **Copyright Search:** While less common, check if the name or any related content is protected by copyright. This is especially important if you plan to use the name in a creative context.
- **Consult a Lawyer:** If you are seriously committed to a name, consider consulting with a lawyer specializing in intellectual property. They can help ensure there won't be legal issues with your chosen name.

Tips for Choosing a Name that Resonates with Your Audience

In addition to being representative and available, your brand name needs to emotionally resonate with your audience. Here are some strategies to achieve that:

- **Connect with Emotions:** Think about the emotions you want to evoke in your customers. Do you want them to feel inspired, empowered, comfortable, or excited? A name that reflects these emotions can help create a stronger connection.
- **Research the Competition:** Look at the names of your competitors. What works and what doesn't? This can give you a sense of how to position your brand and what words or concepts to avoid.
- **Test with Your Audience:** Once you've come up with a few names, consider conducting a small survey among friends, family, or even potential customers. Ask them what each name conveys and which one they like best. External opinions can provide valuable insights.
- **Create a Story Behind the Name:** A name with a story can be more engaging. If you can share the reason behind your choice, customers may feel more connected to your brand. For example, if your name is inspired by a personal experience or a value you hold dear, share that.
- **Stand the Test of Time:** Before making a final decision, imagine how your name will sound in five or ten years. Will it still be relevant? Will you still be proud of it? This will help you choose a name with longevity.

Examples of Successful Brand Names

Here are some examples of brands that have chosen effective names and how those names impacted their success:

- **Nike:** The name comes from the Greek goddess of victory, reflecting aspiration and triumph, which resonates well with their athletic audience.
- **Apple:** A simple and memorable name that suggests simplicity and accessibility, which has been key to their marketing success.
- **Etsy:** A unique name that evokes creativity and artistry, perfectly capturing the essence of what the platform represents.

Practical Exercises

To help you apply what you've learned in this chapter, here are some practical exercises:

- **Brainstorming Session:** Spend 15-20 minutes brainstorming names for your brand. Write down all the names that come to mind without filtering.
- **Name Evaluation:** Select your five favorite names from the list and evaluate them based on simplicity, availability, and emotional connection with your audience.
- **Availability Check:** Use the tools mentioned to check the availability of the selected names in web domains and social media platforms.
- **Consultation and Feedback:** Share your selected names with friends, family, or potential customers and gather their opinions.
- **Story Development:** Write a brief story about why you chose your name. What does it mean to you, and how does it represent your brand?

Conclusion of Chapter 3

Choosing the right name for your brand is a crucial step in creating your company's identity. By following a thoughtful and strategic process, you can find a name that not only represents your brand but also resonates with your audience. Creating an emotional connection and ensuring availability are essential for establishing a strong and memorable brand. Remember, your name is the first impression you give to the world, so take the time to find the perfect one as you move forward in this journey.

4. Logo Design and Creating Visual Identity

A brand's success relies heavily on the design of its logo and the creation of a solid visual identity. These components not only convey your brand's message and values to your audience, but they also help differentiate you in the market. In this chapter, we'll discuss how to design a logo that reflects the essence of your brand, how to choose colors and typography that ensure consistency in your image, and what tools and resources you can use to achieve this.

How to Design a Logo That Reflects Your Brand's Essence

Your logo is the face of your brand and should encapsulate its personality. Here are some steps to create an effective logo:

- **Understand Your Brand's Essence:** Before you begin designing, reflect on your brand's vision and mission (as discussed in Chapter 1). Ask yourself: What emotions do I want to evoke? What values do I want to communicate? A good logo should be a reflection of these aspects.
- **Research the Competition:** Look at the logos of competing brands. Analyze what works and what doesn't in their designs. This will give you insight into industry trends and help you find ways to stand out.
- **Brainstorm Ideas:** Conduct a brainstorming session to generate possible concepts for your logo. Consider images, symbols, or words that represent your brand. Make initial sketches of your ideas without worrying about perfection.
- **Simplicity and Versatility:** An effective logo is often simple and easy to recognize. Think of iconic logos like Nike or Apple; their simplicity is key to their impact. Additionally, ensure your logo is versatile, meaning it should work well in various sizes and on different backgrounds.
- **Design Testing:** Once you have a basic design, test it in multiple formats. Print your logo in different sizes and observe how it looks on various materials (stationery, products, etc.). This will help you spot potential issues with visibility and readability.
- **Feedback:** Share your design with friends, family, or members of your target audience. Ask for feedback on what the logo conveys and whether they think it reflects your brand's essence.
- **Revisions:** Based on the feedback received, make the necessary adjustments. Remember that the design process may require several tweaks before arriving at the final version.

Colors, Typography, and Visual Style: Creating Consistency in Your Brand Image

Once you've designed your logo, the next step is to create a cohesive visual identity that extends to other aspects of your brand.

- **Color Selection:**
  1. The colors you choose have a significant impact on how your brand is perceived. Each color evokes different emotions and associations. For example:
     - **Red:** Energy, passion, action.
     - **Blue:** Trust, calm, security.
     - **Green:** Nature, health, tranquility.
     - **Black:** Elegance, sophistication, power.
  2. Create a color palette that represents your brand's values and personality. Typically, a palette of 2-4 primary colors and some secondary colors works well to maintain consistency while providing enough variety for different applications.
- **Typography:** Typography is crucial, as it also communicates your brand's personality. Decide whether you want a formal or casual, modern or classic style. Ensure that the font is legible across different sizes and platforms. Use a combination of fonts for headings and body text that complement each other and reinforce your brand's tone.
- **Visual Style:** Define your brand's overall visual style, which includes elements like images, patterns, and graphics. This will help create a unified visual experience across all platforms and marketing materials. Consider developing a brand guide that contains guidelines on how to use visual elements to maintain consistency.
- **Examples of Successful Brands:** Analyze successful brands to see how they've built a cohesive visual identity. Notice how they use their colors, typography, and graphic elements across different platforms and products. Brands like Airbnb and Coca-Cola are great examples of how a strong visual identity can influence how a brand is perceived.

Tools and Resources for Logo Design (Professional or DIY)

There are various options to design your logo, ranging from hiring a professional to doing it yourself. Here are some possibilities to consider:

- **Hiring a Graphic Designer:** If your budget allows, working with a professional graphic designer can be the best option. They have the experience and skills to create a logo that perfectly matches your vision. You can find designers on platforms like Upwork, 99designs, or Fiverr. Additionally, you can discover emerging talent on Instagram by searching for ".std" or ".dsg" to find graphic designers showcasing their portfolios.
- **Online Design Tools:** If you're looking for a more budget-friendly approach, there are online tools that let you design your own logo intuitively. Some popular options include:
    - **Canva:** Offers customizable logo templates and is easy to use.
    - **Looka:** Generates logo options based on your preferences.
    - **LogoMaker:** Allows you to quickly create logos with various icons and fonts.
- **Templates and Resources:** Many platforms offer logo templates that you can customize. Additionally, resources like Envato Elements or Creative Market provide graphics, fonts, and elements you can use in your design.
- **Feedback and revision:** Regardless of whether you go DIY or hire a professional, it's essential to get feedback on the final design. This ensures that your logo resonates with your audience and accurately reflects your brand's essence.
- **Prototypes and Testing:** Once you have a final design, create prototypes to see how the logo looks in different applications (website, social media, products). This will help you visualize how it integrates into your overall brand image.

Practical Exercises

To help you apply what you've learned in this chapter, here are some practical exercises:

- **Sketching Ideas:** Draw rough sketches of potential logos using the ideas you've generated. Don't worry about perfection; just let your creativity flow.
- **Creating a Color Palette:** Experiment with different color combinations using tools like Adobe Color. Create at least three palettes and choose the one that best represents your brand.
- **Font Selection:** Test different fonts and create a document with your favorite combinations. Make sure to include options for both headings and body text.
- **Design Feedback:** Show your designs to trusted individuals and gather their opinions. Ask them what emotions each design evokes and whether they think it represents your brand well.
- **Final Revision:** Make adjustments based on the feedback you received, and ensure that your logo and visual elements are consistent across all platforms.

Conclusion of Chapter 4

Creating a visual identity and designing a logo are fundamental steps in establishing your brand in the market. You can build a strong presence that resonates with your audience by reflecting your brand's essence through a well-designed logo, cohesive colors, and appropriate typography. Remember, your visual identity will be the face of your brand, so it's crucial to invest time and effort into its development, whether you choose to design it yourself or hire a professional.

5. Trademark Registration

An important part of creating and protecting your business is registering your trademark. Proper registration safeguards intellectual property rights and strengthens your brand's reputation in the market. This chapter will explain the process of registering a trademark, its importance, how to register both nationally and internationally, the associated costs, and how to protect your name and logo.

Trademark Registration Process: Why Is It Important?
- **Legal Protection:** Registering your trademark grants you exclusive rights to use it, meaning no one else can use a similar name or logo in the same sector. This protects you from potential infringements and legal disputes.
- **Recognition and Trust:** An official registration gives your brand a level of professionalism and credibility. Consumers tend to trust registered brands more, which can enhance the perception of your business.
- **Commercial Value:** A registered trademark can increase your business's value. If you decide to sell your company in the future, having a registered trademark will be a valuable asset.
- **International Rights:** Registering your trademark in your home country is often the first step before expanding internationally, where you'll need to protect your brand to prevent others from using it.
- **Case Study:**
1. **Nike:** Before becoming globally recognized, Nike faced legal challenges with its original name, Blue Ribbon Sports, which was easily confused with other brands. After conducting a search for name availability, they changed their name to "Nike" and registered it, allowing them to operate globally without conflicts.

Costs Associated with Trademark Registration
One of the key aspects to consider is the cost of registering a trademark, which varies by country and the scope of protection (national or international). Here are some approximate examples:
- **United States (USPTO):** Between $225 and $400 per product or service class.
- **European Union (EUIPO):** Approximately €850 per product class.
- **Madrid System (WIPO, for international registration):** Between $600 and $2,000, depending on the number of countries.

It's important to keep in mind that costs can include both the initial application fee and periodic renewal fees required to maintain the trademark.

How to Register Your Trademark Nationally and Internationally

- **National Registration:** The trademark registration process varies by country, but it generally includes the following steps:
    - **Preliminary Search:** Before registering your trademark, conduct a search in the patent and trademark office's database in your country to ensure no similar trademarks are already registered. Some useful platforms include:
        1. **USPTO** (United States)
        2. **EUIPO** (European Union)
        3. **INAPI** (Chile)
        4. **SIC** (Colombia)
        5. **IMPI** (Mexico)
    - **Application Preparation:** Complete the application form, which includes details about your trademark, such as the name, logo, and the products or services you offer.
    - **Filing the Application:** Submit your application to the national trademark office. In most cases, this can be done online.
    - **Examination and Publication:** The office will review your application, and if it meets the requirements, it will be published for opposition, allowing third parties to object if necessary.
    - **Registration:** If no objections are raised, your trademark will be registered, and you will receive a registration certificate.
- **International Registration:** To protect your trademark in multiple countries, you can use the Madrid System, administered by the WIPO (World Intellectual Property Organization). This system allows you to register your trademark in various countries with a single application:
    - **International Application:** File your application with WIPO, indicating the countries where you want to register your trademark.
    - **Examination in Each Country:** Each country will review your application according to its own laws and may either approve or deny the registration.
- **Key Platforms:**
    - **WIPO (OMPI):** The World Intellectual Property Organization for international registrations.
    - **INPI (Brazil):** National office for registration in Brazil.
    - **SIPO (China):** China's intellectual property office.

Practical Steps and Platforms to Protect Your Name and Logo

- **Availability Research:** Use trademark databases to check the availability of your name and logo. Some resources include:
    - **USPTO** for the United States.
    - **EUIPO** for the European Union.
    - **TMView:** An international tool for searching trademarks in over 70 countries.
- **Application Preparation:** Gather all necessary documentation, including the brand name and logo, a description of the products or services, and details on their use.
- **Registration Platforms:** Major platforms for trademark registration include: **USPTO** (USA), **EUIPO** (EU), **WIPO** (International). Many of these offices allow online applications, making the process more convenient.
- **Trademark Renewal:** Keep in mind that trademark registration is not permanent. Generally, you will need to renew it every 10 years (though this timeframe may vary by country). Stay aware of renewal deadlines to avoid expiration.
- **Legal Assistance:** If the process feels overwhelming, consider hiring an intellectual property attorney. They can assist you in completing applications correctly and help you avoid legal issues.
- **Consider Graphic Resources:** On Instagram, you can find graphic designers using tags like ".std" or ".dsg" to hire affordable and personalized services for your logo or visual elements.

Practical Exercises

- **Availability Search:** Conduct a search in your country's trademark database to check if your name and logo are available. Take note of any similar trademarks and evaluate potential conflicts.
- **Prepare Your Application:** Complete a sample application to familiarize yourself with the process, describing your brand, its use, and its distinctive features.
- **Consult a Professional:** Consider scheduling a consultation with an intellectual property attorney, especially if you plan to register your trademark in multiple countries.

Conclusion of Chapter 5

To protect your business and establish a strong presence in the market, it is essential to register your trademark. From legal protection to commercial value, registering your trademark provides the confidence and security needed to grow your business both nationally and internationally. By following the correct procedures, conducting thorough research, and leveraging available resources, you can effectively safeguard your brand.

6. Product Conceptualization

Finding Inspiration for Designs

The first step in conceptualizing your products is finding inspiration. It can come from anywhere: art, nature, cultural trends, or even personal experiences. While researching current fashion trends is helpful, it's crucial that your designs remain unique and reflect your brand's vision and mission.

- **Research Current Trends:** Analyze what's happening in the fashion industry, both globally and locally. Platforms like WGSN, Trendwatching, or fashion magazines such as Vogue and Harper's Bazaar can help you spot emerging patterns and trends.
- **Explore Culture and Art:** Fashion is a reflection of culture. Explore art exhibitions, photography, films, or cultural movements that inspire you. This will not only give you fresh ideas but also help you tell a story through your designs.
- **Inspiration from Nature or Architecture:** Shapes, colors, and textures found in nature or architectural structures can inspire unique designs. Renowned designers like Alexander McQueen found much of their inspiration in nature.
- **Study the Competition:** It's not about copying but learning what works in the market. Observe the type of clothing successful brands in your niche are offering and how you could create an improved or differentiated version.

Practical Tip: Keep a visual journal with images, sketches, and keywords that define your style and what you want to convey through your products. Tools like Pinterest, Instagram, or inspiration boards will allow you to organize your ideas visually.

Working with Designers or Designing on Your Own: Once you have a clear idea, you have two options: hire a professional designer or design the products yourself. If you decide to hire a graphic designer, make sure to communicate your vision clearly by providing examples and visual references.

- **Finding Designers on Social Media:** Platforms like Instagram can be useful for finding graphic designers who include ".std" or ".dsg" in their usernames, indicating they are students or designers. You can reach out to emerging designers who may offer competitive rates.
- **DIY Design Tools:** If you choose to create the designs yourself, you can use software like Adobe Illustrator, Clo 3D, Procreate, or the more accessible Canva, which allows beginners to create basic designs.

Advantages:

- Full control over the creative process.
- Lower development costs.

Disadvantages:

- It can be slower if you lack experience.
- Your designs might not be technically accurate for production.

Creating the Tech Pack: A Key Element

The Tech Pack is an essential tool in the fashion industry, especially when working with manufacturers. It's essentially a detailed document that includes all the necessary information for consistently producing a product.

What is a Tech Pack and Why is it Important?

A Tech Pack is an essential document that ensures your designs are accurately translated into actual products. It serves as a comprehensive guide for manufacturers, explaining all the design details and minimizing errors or misunderstandings. Additionally, it offers legal protection in case of quality issues or contract breaches.

Importance of the Tech Pack:

- **Clear Communication:** Provides detailed descriptions of every design aspect, ensuring the manufacturer understands your expectations.
- **Quality Control:** Establishes a clear standard for finished products, making it easier to verify that the final item meets all requirements.
- **Cost and Time Efficiency:** By minimizing mistakes during production, unnecessary costs are avoided, and delivery times are optimized.

Elements a Tech Pack Should Include

A complete Tech Pack should include:

- **Technical Drawings:** Detailed sketches of the product from all angles.
- **Material Specifications:** Clear descriptions of fabric types, colors, patterns, and other materials.
- **Sizing Guide:** Exact measurements for each size of the product.
- **Production Instructions:** Details on stitching, labels, finishes, and any other technical aspects of the manufacturing process.

Tips for Creating an Effective Tech Pack

- **Be Detailed:** The more information you provide, the more accurate the final product will be.
- **Conduct Preliminary Tests**: Ensure the materials and finishes you include in the Tech Pack work correctly before production.
- **Use Specialized Software:** Platforms like Techpacker make it easier to create Tech Packs in a structured and efficient way.

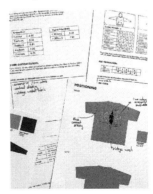

Developing Your First Collection: What to Consider:

When designing your first collection, it's important that the products you develop align with your brand's vision while also being marketable. Here are some key factors to consider:

- **Create a Cohesive Collection:** While offering different products is fine, ensure they all share a common style. This reinforces your brand identity and makes the collection feel unified.
- **Limited Variety, Big Impact:** Start with a few products but make sure each one offers something unique. This allows you to manage costs while still capturing customer interest.

How to Ensure Your Products Reflect Your Brand Vision

Your collection should speak for itself. The choice of materials, colors, and design details should be consistent with your brand identity. For instance, if your brand focuses on sustainability, this should be reflected through the use of organic or recycled materials.

- **Consider Sustainability and Ethics:** There's currently a high demand for sustainable products. Consider including ethical and responsible elements, such as eco-friendly materials, and be sure to communicate these efforts to your customers.

Additional Strategies to Strengthen Your Collection

- **Market Trend Research:** Staying updated on industry trends will help you design products that resonate with what consumers are looking for, without sacrificing the authenticity of your brand.
- **Test with Your Audience:** Before mass-producing, you can create a small batch or even use platforms like Kickstarter or Indiegogo to validate your collection and gather feedback.
- **Limited or Capsule Collections:** Creating limited-edition collections can generate a sense of urgency, making customers feel like they're getting exclusive products. This strategy also helps control costs and prevents overproduction.
- **Gather Customer Feedback:** Especially for your first collection, receiving customer feedback and constructive criticism is crucial to improving future products.

Conclusion of Chapter 6

One of the most creative and exciting steps in building your clothing brand is product conceptualization. Each part of the process brings you closer to turning your ideas into reality, from finding inspiration to working on the creation of the Tech Pack. Every aspect of your product, from the initial design to the technical details, should reflect your brand's values and vision.

By following a well-structured process, you can ensure that your products are not only visually appealing but also technically viable and of high quality. The key lies in clearly defining what you want your brand to communicate and working effectively with designers and suppliers so that every garment embodies that vision.

This chapter emphasizes the importance of the Tech Pack as the main guide for ensuring consistency and quality in production, equipping you with the tools and knowledge to turn your ideas into tangible products. You'll be prepared to confidently enter the market and stand out in the fashion industry with a well-conceptualized first collection.

7. Suppliers and Production

After having your designs and Tech Pack ready, the next step is finding reliable suppliers who can bring your ideas to life. This chapter addresses the process of selecting suppliers, the importance of samples, how to negotiate prices and deadlines, and the advantages and challenges of producing in small quantities.

How and Where to Find Reliable Suppliers

The success of your brand largely depends on the quality of your products, and to ensure that quality, it's essential to choose reliable and experienced suppliers. Below, we explore some places and strategies to find good suppliers.

- **Online Platforms:** Nowadays, there are numerous platforms that allow you to access suppliers worldwide. Some of the most well-known are:
1. **Alibaba:** One of the most popular platforms for finding manufacturers worldwide, especially in Asia. You can filter suppliers by categories, read reviews, and compare prices.
2. **Global Sources:** Similar to Alibaba, but with a more selective focus and additional supplier verification.
3. **Faire:** A platform more oriented towards handmade products and small producers, ideal if you're looking for more personalized, small-scale production.
4. **Maker's Row:** Popular in the U.S., it connects manufacturers and designers with local factories.

- **Trade Shows:**

Attending fashion and textile trade shows is a great way to meet suppliers in person. Some well-known trade shows include:
1. **Première Vision (París):** Ideal for finding high-quality suppliers for fabrics, materials, and manufacturing.
2. **Texworld USA:** A textile and apparel trade show in New York that connects designers with international manufacturers.
3. **Magic (Las Vegas):** One of the largest trade shows in the U.S., where you can meet suppliers, discover new trends, and network.

- **Local Contacts**

Don't underestimate the importance of searching for local or regional manufacturers. While it may be more expensive than producing in Asian countries, having a nearby supplier makes it easier to oversee the production process, communicate effectively, and reduce shipping times.

Requesting Samples: What to Check Before Confirming Production

Requesting a sample of your product is one of the most critical steps in this process. Samples allow you to verify the quality of the material, stitching, color, and manufacturing details before committing to mass production.

- **Quality Review**

When you receive the sample, carefully evaluate the following aspects:

1. **Material:** Ensure the supplier is using the materials specified in the Tech Pack. Feel the fabric, stretch it, and make sure it meets your expectations.
2. **Stitching:** Stitching is a clear indicator of manufacturing quality. Check if the seams are aligned and reinforced in key areas such as the shoulders or pockets.
3. **Finishes:** Pay attention to details such as buttons, zippers, labels, and any other added components. They should be firmly attached and of good quality.
4. **Color and Print:** Ensure that the colors match what you specified. Check if the prints are well-placed and not distorted.

- **Product Testing**

Try the product yourself or have people who represent your target customer try it on. Check the fit, comfort, and how the material behaves after washing. A product that loses its shape or color after a few washes can damage your brand's reputation.

- **Corrections and Adjustments**

It's common for the first sample not to be perfect. This is normal, but be sure to provide detailed feedback and request corrections until the sample fully meets your expectations.

Price and Deadline Negotiation

Once you're satisfied with the sample, it's time to negotiate prices and deadlines. This is crucial to ensure that your production is profitable and delivered on time. Here are some strategies for effective negotiation:

- **Negotiation Strategies**
1. **Order Volume:** Manufacturers often offer lower prices for larger quantities. If you're just starting out, you can negotiate a moderate price and agree on discounts as your volume increases.
2. **Flexibility in Deadlines:** If you can be flexible with delivery times, you may negotiate better rates. Suppliers often adjust their prices based on the urgency of the order.
3. **Stage Payments:** Instead of paying everything upfront, negotiate payments in stages. An initial payment before production starts, another halfway through, and the final payment when production is complete. This ensures that both sides are committed to the process.

- **Hidden Costs**

In addition to the cost per unit, make sure to ask about additional costs, such as:

1. **Shipping fees.**
2. **Customs duties or taxes.**
3. **Charges for additional quality testing.**

Producing in Small Quantities: Advantages and Challenges

When starting out, many brands choose to produce in small quantities to minimize risks. This strategy has both advantages and challenges that you should consider.

Advantages

- **Lower Initial Investment:** Producing in small quantities allows you to better manage your cash flow since you're not investing all your capital in large amounts of inventory.
- **Flexibility:** You can adjust the product and strategy based on initial sales. If something isn't working, you can pivot without having to get rid of large amounts of stock.
- **Generating Exclusivity:** Producing limited or capsule collections creates a sense of urgency among consumers, which can increase demand.

Challenges

- **Higher Costs per Unit:** Suppliers typically charge more for small productions since fixed costs are spread over fewer units.
- **Limited Stock:** If you underestimate demand, you could run out of inventory quickly, which may frustrate your customers.
- **Difficulty in Negotiation:** With smaller volumes, it's harder to negotiate significant discounts on the price per unit or delivery times.

Solutions to Minimize Risks

- **Market Testing:** Before committing to mass production, conduct small-scale tests. This will allow you to gauge demand and adjust your strategy accordingly.
- **Partnering with Multiple Suppliers:** Having several suppliers lets you compare prices and options, plus you'll have a backup plan in case one falls through.
- **Crowdfunding:** Platforms like Kickstarter allow the public to fund your first production, ensuring you don't produce more than you need while generating interest in your product.

Conclusion of Chapter 7

The production process and supplier selection are critical parts of building your clothing brand. To ensure the quality and success of your collection, you need to choose a reliable supplier, request samples, and negotiate effectively. While producing in small quantities lets you be agile and minimize risks, it also requires careful management of costs and demand. With the right strategies and tools, you'll be able to create a collection that reflects your brand's vision and meets your customers' expectations.

8. Prototype Creation and Quality Control

Prototype creation and quality control are the next critical steps to ensure that your product meets expectations after securing a reliable supplier and negotiating production terms. This chapter explains what to expect from the initial samples and how to implement effective quality control before moving on to final production.

Sample Creation Process and Adjustments

The initial prototype or sample is your first tangible approach to the final product. This process is essential to ensure that the conceptual design you've created in your Tech Pack translates correctly into a physical product.

- **Development of the First Sample**

Developing the prototype is a critical step, as it's where you'll see your ideas come to life for the first time. Here are some important steps in this process:

1. **Clear Communication with the Supplier:** Ensure that your supplier has access to all relevant information, including details like materials, measurements, colors, and finishes. This is where your Tech Pack plays a key role; it should be clear and detailed.
2. **Material Selection:** The materials you choose are vital to the quality of your product. Make sure your suppliers are using the specified materials, and if necessary, test various alternatives to find the best combination of quality and cost.
3. **Time and Cost:** Prototype creation can be time-consuming and, depending on the complexity of the design, may be costly. Don't underestimate how long it may take to get the perfect sample; multiple adjustments and revisions are often required.

- **Review and Adjustments of the Sample**

The first sample is almost never perfect. After receiving the initial prototype, you'll need to thoroughly review it and make adjustments as necessary. Here's how to conduct this review:

1. **Design Adjustment:** Assess the fit of the garment or product. If something doesn't fit correctly, make sure to adjust the measurements or pattern as needed.
2. **Material Verification:** Check that the materials are correct and provide the desired quality. Does the fabric have the right feel, weight, and drape? Does the print or embroidery look as you expected?
3. **Detail Review:** Small details like seams, labels, and closures should meet your expectations. Ensure they are correctly placed and durable.
4. **Wear Testing:** Conduct wear and wash tests to see how the product holds up after several uses. This will help you identify potential issues like fading, shrinkage, or weak seams.

Providing detailed feedback to your supplier is crucial, explaining each adjustment you want to implement so they can make the necessary changes.

- **Second Round of Samples**

It's common to request a second (or even third) round of prototypes after the first sample. This process may seem lengthy, but it's essential for achieving a final product that meets your brand's quality standards.

What to Expect from the First Prototypes

The prototyping process can be exciting but also frustrating. It's important to have realistic expectations and be prepared to make adjustments.

- **Initial Imperfections:** It's completely normal for the first prototype to not be perfect. Issues may arise with fit, materials, colors, or construction details. Don't be discouraged if this happens. These imperfections are an expected part of the process and give you the opportunity to improve the product before its launch.
- **Iteration Time:** Depending on the complexity of your design and your supplier's experience, the time needed to adjust a prototype can vary. This process can take weeks or even months, so it's essential to include enough buffer time in your overall planning. Additionally, remember that making changes to the pattern or design may increase the cost of the samples, so it's important to be prepared for these financial adjustments.
- **Ongoing Communication:** Keep an open and constant line of communication with your supplier throughout the prototyping process. A good supplier will allow you to ask questions and provide regular updates on the status of the prototype. The smoother the communication, the quicker you can make necessary adjustments and move toward final production.

Ensuring Quality Before Final Production

Ensuring the quality of your product is one of the most important aspects before giving the green light for mass production. Without rigorous quality control, you risk producing defective products, which can lead to returns, customer dissatisfaction, and damage to your brand's reputation.

- **Quality Standards**

You must establish clear quality standards that include details about materials, measurements, construction techniques, and finishes. These standards should align with what you expect from your final product and what you offer your customers. Key areas to review include:

1. **Durability:** Ensure that seams are strong and that the garments or products can withstand prolonged use.
2. **Fit and Size Accuracy:** Verify that the size and fit are consistent and accurate as specified in the Tech Pack.
3. **Finishes:** Details such as buttons, zippers, labels, and embroidery should be properly placed and secured.

- **Final Sample Inspection**

Once you have an approved final sample, conduct a detailed inspection. Make sure it meets all the requirements outlined in your Tech Pack and that any previous issues have been resolved.

- **Quality Control During Production**

Implementing a quality control process during production is crucial. This can include conducting periodic inspections at the factory or establishing quality control checkpoints with the supplier. Some strategies for ensuring good quality control include:

1. **Random Product Inspection:** Randomly inspect a specific number of finished products to ensure they all meet the same standards.
2. **Stress Testing:** Conduct tension and durability tests on seams, buttons, or closures to ensure the product can withstand daily use.
3. **Monitoring Each Batch:** If you're producing in multiple rounds or batches, ensure each one maintains the same quality standards.

- **External Quality Control**

Some brands choose to hire an external quality control team to conduct audits at the factory during production. This team can provide an impartial assessment and ensure that the products you receive meet your expectations.

Conclusion of Chapter 8

The creation of prototypes and quality control are crucial stages in developing a successful clothing brand. By implementing a careful review process and rigorous quality control, you can ensure that your products reflect your brand's vision and meet your customers' expectations. Although the process may be slow and filled with changes, it is an important investment to ensure that your final collection is of the highest quality and ready to compete with others in the fashion market.

9. Budgeting and Financial Management

The success of any clothing brand relies on budgeting and financial management. Good financial planning and proper cost control will help you keep the business running, avoid overspending, and achieve profitability. In this chapter, you'll learn how to allocate your initial budget, reduce costs without sacrificing quality, estimate profit margins, and avoid financial issues during the early stages of your brand.

Initial Budget: How to Allocate Resources

One of the biggest challenges when starting a clothing brand is efficiently allocating limited resources. In the beginning, you'll likely have a tight budget, so it's essential to know how to distribute it among various key areas. Here are the main components to consider when allocating your budget:

- **Design:**
1. Costs for hiring graphic and fashion designers or investing in design tools if you decide to do it yourself.
2. Creating the Tech Pack: the costs of producing a complete and detailed tech pack can vary, but it's a key investment to ensure production quality.
3. Expenses for initial samples.
- **Production:**
4. Manufacturing costs for garments, including both materials and labor.
5. Expenses for creating prototypes and small-batch production before scaling up.
6. Transportation and logistics, which are essential for sourcing materials and distributing your products.
- **Marketing and Branding:**
7. Investment in digital marketing, social media advertising, and creating visual content like photos and videos of your products.
8. Expenses for creating a professional website and online store, as well as subscriptions to e-commerce platforms or digital marketing tools.
9. Costs for designing the logo and other elements of your brand's visual identity.
- **Operations and Logistics:**
10. Inventory management and storage if you decide to handle stock on your own.
11. Shipping costs for deliveries to customers, both domestic and international.

Distributing the budget evenly, without neglecting any of these areas, is vital for a solid start.

Cost Reduction Without Sacrificing Quality

One of the biggest challenges when launching a clothing brand is balancing cost control with product quality. Reducing costs smartly can be key to your brand's success without negatively affecting customers' perception of your brand. Here are some strategies to keep costs low without compromising quality:

- **Produce in Small Quantities:** Although producing in large quantities is usually cheaper per unit, starting out with small batches is more sensible. This allows you to test the market without making a massive investment that could go unsold.
- **Negotiate with Suppliers:** Building a good relationship with your suppliers is essential. Often, negotiations can lead to discounts, better payment terms, or lower production rates.
- **Simplify Design:** Sometimes, small changes in design can significantly reduce production costs. Opt for designs that use materials efficiently and don't require complicated manufacturing processes, without losing the essence of your brand.
- **Outsource Non-Essential Processes:** Instead of spending on infrastructure and in-house staff, consider outsourcing services like accounting, marketing, or shipping management.

Estimating Profit Margins

A crucial part of financial management is knowing how to estimate and calculate your profit margins to ensure that your brand is profitable. Here are some key guidelines for accurately estimating your margins:

- **Total Costs per Unit:** This includes all costs related to producing a garment, from materials to transportation and storage costs. Be sure to include hidden expenses like returns, shipping costs, and sales platform commissions.
- **Selling Price:** Once you know the total production cost, decide on your selling price. This should align with your brand strategy and market prices. A typical profit margin in the fashion industry ranges from 50% to 70%.
- **Gross Margin:** The gross profit margin is calculated by subtracting the production cost from the selling price and dividing that value by the selling price. For example, if it costs you €20 to produce a garment and you sell it for €50, your margin would be 60%.

How to Avoid Financial Problems in the Early Stages

During the first few months, it's easy to make financial mistakes that could jeopardize your brand's success. Here are some recommendations to avoid financial issues:

- **Control Expenses:** Keep a detailed record of all expenses from day one. Having a solid accounting system will allow you to identify areas where you might be overspending and make adjustments before they become problems.
- **Don't Underestimate Hidden Costs:** Many entrepreneurs forget to accurately calculate hidden costs such as marketing, product returns, and technology expenses. Make sure to have a financial cushion to cover these unforeseen circumstances.
- **Strategically Reinvest:** In the early stages, it's tempting to spend all profits on expansion, but it's crucial to reinvest only what's necessary and maintain a reserve of funds for contingencies.
- **Avoid Overestimating Production:** Resist the temptation to produce large quantities right from the start. Starting with small batches not only allows you to assess demand but also protects you from having large amounts of unsold inventory.
- **Seek Financing if Necessary:** If your brand begins to grow rapidly and you need more capital, don't hesitate to explore financing options such as investors, small business loans, or crowdfunding platforms.

Conclusion of Chapter 9

The success of your clothing brand will depend on financial management and budget planning. With an efficient allocation of resources, controlled production, and a strategic focus on quality and price, you will be prepared to avoid common mistakes that could jeopardize your business. The key is to make financial decisions based on solid data and a realistic projection of your brand's growth while maintaining a balance between investment and return.

10. Creating a Website for Your Brand

Importance of Having Your Own Online Store
In the digital age, having an online store is not just an option; it's a necessity. A dedicated website provides a platform to showcase your products, tell your brand's story, and connect directly with your customers. Some key benefits include:

- **24/7 Accessibility:** Unlike a physical store, an online shop allows customers to explore and purchase your products at any time, which can increase your sales.
- **Total Control Over Your Brand:** With your own website, you can customize the customer experience, from design to content, ensuring that your brand is authentically reflected.
- **Data Analytics:** Online stores offer analytical tools that track user behavior, helping you make informed decisions about your marketing and sales strategies.
- **Market Expansion:** An online store allows you to reach customers worldwide, significantly broadening your potential customer base.

Platforms for Creating Your Website
Choosing the right platform for your online store is crucial. Here are some of the most popular options:

- **Shopify:** Ideal for beginners, Shopify is an all-in-one platform that provides everything you need to create and manage your online store. It features a wide range of customizable templates, payment integrations, and marketing tools.
- **WordPress:** With the WooCommerce plugin, WordPress becomes a powerful e-commerce platform. It's more flexible and scalable, making it ideal if you plan to grow and expand your site in the future, although it may require a bit more technical knowledge.
- **Wix:** With a drag-and-drop interface, Wix is user-friendly and allows you to create an attractive website without any coding knowledge. However, it may be less flexible than Shopify or WordPress in terms of customizing specific functionalities.

Web Design: Tips for an Attractive and Functional Online Store

The design of your website is crucial for capturing the attention of visitors and converting them into customers. Consider these aspects:

- **Responsive Design:** Ensure that your website looks good and functions properly on mobile devices, as more people are shopping from their phones.
- **Intuitive Navigation:** Organize your products into clear categories and use an easy-to-navigate menu. Ease of navigation is key to providing a good user experience.
- **High-Quality Images:** Use professional photographs that showcase your products from different angles. Quality images can significantly influence the purchase decision.
- **Clear Calls to Action (CTA):** Incorporate clear call-to-action buttons, such as "Add to Cart" or "Buy Now," to guide users through the purchasing process.
- **Testimonials and Reviews:** Include customer reviews to enhance your brand's credibility and provide social proof that motivates others to buy.

Integration of Payment Methods and Logistics Solutions

Facilitating the purchasing process is essential to minimize cart abandonment. Consider the following:

- **Payment Methods:** Offer multiple payment options, such as credit cards, PayPal, and mobile payment services like Apple Pay and Google Pay. This provides convenience to customers and can increase the conversion rate.
- **Logistics:** Partner with reliable shipping companies and offer various shipping options (standard, express, etc.) to meet your customers' needs. Additionally, ensure that your site includes clear shipping and return policies.

Basic SEO to Increase Your Brand's Visibility

SEO (Search Engine Optimization) is essential for making your online store visible on the web. Here are some basic practices:

- **Keywords:** Research and use relevant keywords in your product descriptions, titles, and tags. This will help your products be found more easily by search engines.
- **Quality Content:** Publish useful and relevant content on your blog, such as style guides or brand stories, that can attract organic traffic and improve your SEO.
- **Image Optimization:** Ensure that all images of your products are optimized (appropriate size and ALT tags) to improve site loading speed and visibility in image searches.
- **Internal Links:** Use internal links to direct visitors to other parts of your site, such as related products, thereby increasing the duration of visits and opportunities for purchases.

- **Technical Aspects**
1. **Choosing a Domain:** Pick a domain name that is easy to remember and reflects your brand. A good domain is crucial for the identity of your online store.
2. **Loading Speed:** Ensure that your website loads quickly, as a slow site can frustrate users and lead to higher cart abandonment rates.
3. **Site Security:** Implement an SSL certificate to protect your customers' data and build trust in your online store.
- **Digital Marketing Strategies**
4. **Social Media Use:** Promote your online store through platforms like Instagram, Facebook, and Pinterest, where you can showcase your products and connect with your customers.
5. **Email Marketing:** Use email marketing campaigns to keep customers informed about new collections, promotions, and brand news.
6. **Online Advertising:** Consider investing in Google Ads and social media advertising to increase the visibility of your store and attract targeted traffic.
- **Optimizing the Sales Funnel**
7. **Retargeting:** Use retargeting strategies to bring back visitors who abandoned their carts, reminding them of the products they left behind.
8. **Cart Abandonment Recovery:** Implement email reminders to encourage customers to complete their purchases.
- **Results Analysis**
9. **Analytical Tools:** Use tools like Google Analytics to monitor your website's performance by analyzing key metrics such as conversion rates, time spent on the site, and user behavior.
10. **Continuous Improvement:** Based on the data collected, adjust your marketing strategy and user experience to continuously improve.
- **Legal Aspects**
11. **E-commerce Regulations:** Ensure compliance with e-commerce laws and regulations, such as data protection and consumer privacy, by including clear privacy policies and terms of service on your site.

Conclusion of Chapter 10

Creating a website for your clothing brand is an essential step toward success in today's market. By focusing on accessibility, attractive design, payment method integration, and search engine optimization, you can establish a strong online presence that attracts customers and converts them into loyal buyers. With proper planning and execution, your online store will become a powerful tool for achieving your business goals and growing your brand.

11. Digital Marketing Strategies

In today's world, digital marketing is crucial for the growth and visibility of any brand, especially in the fashion industry. A well-defined strategy can attract your target audience, increase sales, and build a loyal customer base. Below, we discuss the best digital marketing strategies you can use to expand your clothing brand.

Creating Content for Social Media
Quality content is key to capturing your audience's attention and keeping them engaged. Here are some tips on how to create compelling content:

- **Know Your Audience:** Research who your potential customers are, their interests, and their behaviors on social media. This will help you create content that resonates with them.
- **Types of Content:** Vary the content you share to keep your audience interested. Consider including the following:
1. **Product Images:** Showcase your clothing in an attractive way, using different angles and settings.
2. **Behind-the-Scenes:** Share the process of creating your products, highlighting the authenticity of your brand.
3. **Educational Content:** Publish style guides, fashion tips, or information about sustainability in the industry, demonstrating your knowledge and passion for the subject.
4. **Customer Testimonials:** Share reviews and photos of satisfied customers wearing your products, which helps build trust in your brand.
- **Content Calendar:** Create an editorial calendar to help you plan and organize your posts. This ensures a consistent presence on social media and allows you to prepare campaigns around important events or launches.

How to Leverage Instagram, TikTok, and Other Platforms to Promote Your Brand

Social platforms like Instagram and TikTok are essential for fashion brands as they allow you to visually showcase your products and connect authentically with your audience. Here are some strategies for each platform:

- **Instagram:**
1. **Stories and Reels:** Use stories for short-lived content and Reels to create short, engaging videos that showcase your products in action. Reels have high organic reach potential.
2. **Product Tags:** Take advantage of the product tagging feature in posts and stories, allowing users to shop directly from your content.
3. **Community Engagement:** Respond to comments and direct messages, create polls and questions in stories to encourage participation, and build a closer relationship with your followers.
- **TikTok:**
4. **Challenges and Trends:** Participate in popular challenges and trends, adapting them to your brand. This can increase your brand's visibility and attract new followers.
5. **Behind-the-Scenes Videos:** Share videos that show the creation, packaging, and shipping process of your products, humanizing your brand and fostering emotional connections.
6. **Collaborations with Creators:** Partner with relevant content creators on TikTok to expand your reach and visibility.
- **Pinterest:**
7. **Themed Boards:** Create boards that reflect different styles or collections of your brand, using high-quality images to attract users looking for fashion inspiration.
8. **Direct Links to Products:** Ensure that each pin includes a direct link to your online store, making it easier for users to shop.

Collaborations with Influencers and Micro-Influencers

Collaborating with influencers can significantly increase your brand's visibility and help you reach new audiences. Consider these points:

- **Identifying influencers:** Research and choose influencers who align with your brand's values and aesthetics. Micro-influencers, who have between 1,000 and 100,000 followers, often have higher engagement rates and may be more accessible for collaboration.
- **Types of Collaboration:**
1. **Sponsored Posts:** Ask influencers to create posts wearing or using your products, offering monetary compensation or free products in return.
2. **Social Media Takeover:** Allow an influencer to take over your social media accounts for a day, showcasing how they use your products and sharing their personal style.
3. **Live Events:** Host live events where influencers present your products to their audience, creating real-time interaction and engagement.
- **Measuring Results:** After collaborations, assess their effectiveness by tracking metrics like click-through rates, follower growth, and sales generated.

Paid vs. Organic Advertising: Which is Better for Starting Out?

Both paid and organic advertising have advantages, and the best choice depends on your goals and resources.

- **Paid Advertising:**
1. **Immediate Reach:** Paid campaigns (e.g., Facebook Ads, Instagram Ads) can quickly generate visibility, which is helpful if you need to drive traffic immediately.
2. **Targeting Precision:** You can target specific audiences based on interests, demographics, and behaviors, which can be highly effective.
3. **Cost:** Paid advertising may require a significant investment, especially at the beginning, so it's important to set a clear budget.
- **Organic Advertising:**
4. **Long-Term Growth:** Building an audience organically is often slower, but it can lead to more sustainable growth in the long term.
5. **Low Cost:** It doesn't require spending money on ads, though it does involve investing time and effort in creating valuable content and engaging with your audience.
6. **Authenticity:** Organic content is often perceived as more genuine, which can foster stronger emotional connections with your followers.

Conclusion of Chapter 11

The success of a clothing brand relies heavily on digital marketing strategies. Your brand's visibility and emotional connection with your audience depend on every step, from creating engaging social media content to collaborating with influencers. By carefully considering the right mix of paid and organic advertising, you can make a significant impact in the market and maximize your reach. By consistently applying these strategies, you'll see your brand begin to grow and thrive in the competitive fashion world.

12 Logistics, Inventory, and Shipping Management

The success of your clothing brand depends on logistics, shipping, and inventory management. An effective approach in these areas can reduce costs, improve customer experience, and increase sales. Let's dive into each of these crucial aspects.

How to Manage Inventory Without Overloading Your Budget

Proper inventory management is essential to maintain the financial health of your brand. Here are some tips to achieve that:

- **Establish an Inventory Management System:** Consider using specialized inventory management software that helps you track stock, sales, and orders. Tools like TradeGecko or Cin7 can be useful for small brands.
- **Forecast Demand:** Analyze past sales and market trends to anticipate demand. This will allow you to make informed decisions about how much product to keep in stock.
- **Start with Small Quantities:** Especially early on, opt for small production batches. This helps you assess demand without overextending your budget, allowing flexibility to adjust production based on what works.
- **Implement an Inventory Management Method:** Consider using the FIFO (First In, First Out) method to ensure that older products are sold first, minimizing the risk of obsolescence.
- **Perform Regular Audits:** Set up a schedule to review and audit your inventory regularly. This helps you quickly identify discrepancies and ensure that your stock aligns with sales.

Logistics Solutions for Small Brands

Logistics can be challenging, especially for small brands just starting out. Here are some solutions to consider:

- **Fulfillment Centers:** Outsourcing logistics to a fulfillment center can be a good option. These companies handle storage, order preparation, and shipping. Examples include ShipBob, Red Stag Fulfillment, or Fulfillment by Amazon (FBA). This allows you to focus on growing your brand without worrying about logistics.
- **Dropshipping:** If you want to further reduce inventory costs, consider dropshipping. With this model, you don't need to store products; instead, shipping is handled directly from the supplier to the end customer.
- **In-House Storage:** If your sales volume is low, you can start by managing inventory from home. Make sure to have a designated space to organize products and make them easily accessible.
- **Logistics Planning:** Whenever possible, plan your shipments in advance. Maintain an open relationship with logistics providers and consider the possibility of volume discounts.

Packaging and Presentation: Details That Make a Difference

The presentation of your products is crucial for customer experience. Good packaging not only protects the product but also reinforces your brand identity. Here are some recommendations:

- **Use Quality Materials:** Choose sturdy and attractive boxes and wrapping. Consider sustainability by selecting eco-friendly materials, which can also attract environmentally conscious customers.
- **Personalize Your Packaging:** Incorporate your logo and brand colors into the packaging. Consider adding details like custom seals or tags to make unboxing a memorable experience for the customer.
- **Include Personalized Notes:** A handwritten note or thank-you card can make customers feel valued and appreciated, fostering loyalty.
- **Ensure Product Safety:** Use adequate protective materials (like bubble wrap or tissue paper) to ensure products arrive in perfect condition.

Platforms for Efficient Shipping Management

Choosing the right platform to manage your shipments can streamline the process and enhance customer satisfaction. Here are some options to consider:

- **ShipStation:** This platform allows you to manage multiple carriers and automate shipping processes, making it easier to track orders and handle shipping labels.
- **Easyship:** Offers tools to calculate shipping rates, generate labels, and manage international fulfillment, making it ideal if you plan to sell in global markets.
- **Pirate Ship:** A free option that simplifies the shipping process and provides discounted shipping rates.
- **Shopify Shipping:** If you use Shopify as your sales platform, its shipping feature allows you to manage everything from one place, including printing labels and tracking packages.

Conclusion of Chapter 12

The success of a clothing brand depends on logistics, inventory, and shipping management. By optimizing operations and enhancing the customer experience through effective inventory management, selecting the best logistical solutions, and presenting your products attractively, you can improve efficiency. Choosing the right shipping platforms ensures timely deliveries and perfect product conditions, increasing customer loyalty and helping your brand grow.

13. Brand Launch

The launch of your brand is a significant milestone in your entrepreneurial journey. All the planning, design, and production efforts culminate at this moment, and how you execute this launch can determine your brand's success. This chapter will cover successful launch strategies, creating anticipation, and managing initial sales and feedback.

Strategies for a Successful Launch
For your launch to be successful, it's essential to implement a well-structured strategy that includes the following aspects:

- **Define Your Value Proposition:** Ensure your audience clearly understands what makes your brand unique and why they should choose your products over the competition. This could include quality, design, sustainability, or the message you convey.
- **Create a Launch Campaign:** Plan a marketing campaign that spans multiple platforms. This can include social media ads, blog content, press releases, and email marketing campaigns. Ensure that all messages are consistent and reflect your brand's identity.
- **Set a Launch Date:** Select a launch date and make sure to promote it adequately. You could create an online event, such as an Instagram Live or a Facebook Event, where followers can interact with you and learn more about your brand and products.
- **Strategic Collaborations:** Consider collaborating with influencers or micro-influencers who align with your brand's values. This can help you reach new audiences and build trust from the start.
- **Prepare Your Website:** Ensure your website is ready for launch. Conduct thorough testing to verify that all links work, the checkout process is smooth, and the user experience is optimal.

Creating Anticipation: The Power of Pre-Launch

Anticipation can be a powerful ally when launching your brand. Here are some tactics to create excitement:

- **Social Media Teasers:** Post teaser content on your social media that generates curiosity without revealing too much. This could include blurry product photos, intriguing messages, or a countdown to the launch.
- **Email Lists and Early Promotions:** Invite your followers to sign up for an email list to receive updates about the launch. Offer exclusive promotions or discounts for those who register, creating a sense of urgency.
- **Product Samples:** Consider sending samples to influencers or select customers before the launch. This not only builds anticipation but also provides testimonials and valuable content you can use in your launch campaign.
- **Engagement on Social Media:** Keep your audience engaged through polls, questions, or contests that allow them to interact with the brand before its launch.

Tips for Managing Initial Sales and Feedback

Once you've launched your brand, it's essential to effectively manage initial sales and feedback:

- **Exceptional Customer Service:** From day one, ensure you provide outstanding customer service. Respond quickly to inquiries, handle complaints empathetically, and show your customers that you value their experience.
- **Request Feedback:** Encourage your customers to leave comments about their purchases. You can send email surveys or ask for reviews on social media. This feedback is invaluable for improving your products and customer experience.
- **Analyze Sales and Trends:** Closely monitor sales and customer behavior. Analyze which products are selling best and adjust your marketing and production strategy accordingly.
- **Adjustments and Improvements:** Don't hesitate to make changes based on feedback. If you receive comments about a specific aspect of your products or service, take it as an opportunity to improve and adapt.
- **Celebrate Success:** Reach milestones, such as your first sale or the first 100 orders, and share these achievements with your audience. Celebrating these moments fosters an emotional connection with your community and encourages loyalty.

Conclusion of Chapter 13

The thrilling moment of launching your brand demands careful planning and execution. By implementing effective strategies, creating anticipation, and managing initial sales and feedback properly, you can lay the groundwork for future success. Remember that every interaction with your customers is an opportunity to build your reputation and establish a strong relationship, which will be essential for the long-term growth and sustainability of your brand.

14. Growth and Scalability

Any clothing brand aiming for long-term success needs to grow and scale. This chapter will focus on reinvesting profits, when and how to increase production, diversification strategies, and a gradual expansion plan based on revenue.

Reinvesting Profits to Scale Your Brand
Reinvesting profits is a key strategy for growth. Here are some ways to do it:

- **Evaluate Performance:** Before reinvesting, it's essential to analyze your brand's performance. Review your sales figures, profit margins, and operating costs. Understanding your numbers will help identify areas where reinvestment will have the most significant impact.
- **Allocate a Percentage of Profits:** Decide on a specific percentage of your profits that you will reinvest. This could be 20% or more, depending on your needs and goals. The key is to be consistent and have a clear plan for these funds.
- **Invest in Marketing:** Consider investing in digital marketing campaigns and social media content development. Increased visibility can translate to more sales and greater brand recognition.
- **Enhance Infrastructure:** Use part of the profits to improve your infrastructure. This may include updating your website, enhancing logistics and shipping, or investing in tools that optimize inventory management.
- **Training and Development:** Continuous education is crucial. Invest in yourself and your team through training courses, workshops, and seminars that help improve your skills and knowledge in the industry.

When and How to Increase Production

Knowing when and how to increase production is essential for meeting demand without compromising quality. Here are some points to consider:

- **Analyze Demand:** Monitor sales trends and customer feedback. If you notice a consistent increase in demand, it's a good time to consider scaling up production. Use analytical tools to help forecast future demand.
- **Evaluate Production Capacity:** Before increasing production, assess your current capacity. Ensure that your suppliers and team can handle the increase without sacrificing quality.
- **Gradual Increases:** Increase production gradually rather than making a big leap. This will allow you to evaluate how the market responds and adjust your production accordingly. For example, if you currently produce 100 units of a product and demand is high, consider increasing to 150 units and observe the response.
- **Maintain Quality:** Quality should not be compromised when increasing production. Establish strict quality control measures and ensure that your team is trained to manage the additional production effectively.

Diversification Strategies: New Garments and Collections

Diversifying your product line can be an effective way to grow. Here are some strategies to consider:

- **Research Market Trends:** Stay updated on market trends and consumer preferences. Investigate what types of garments are popular and how you can incorporate them into your line.
- **Test New Products:** Consider launching a limited line of new products to gauge market acceptance. This will allow you to gather feedback and make adjustments before scaling up production.
- **Launch Themed Collections:** Develop collections that follow a specific theme or concept. This can create excitement around your brand and attract different segments of your audience.
- **Collaborations:** Collaborate with other designers or brands to create limited editions. This not only diversifies your line but can also attract new customers who are followers of your collaborators.
- **Innovation in Materials and Designs:** Don't be afraid to experiment with new materials and designs. Innovation can set you apart from the competition and attract a broader audience.

Gradual Expansion Plan Based on Revenue

A gradual expansion plan based on revenue is essential for sustainable growth. Here are some steps to follow:

- **Set Revenue Goals:** Define clear and achievable revenue goals for each quarter or year. This will help you measure your progress and establish milestones for your expansion.
- **Review and Adjust the Plan:** Regularly review your results and adjust your plan as necessary. If you exceed your expectations, consider accelerating your expansion process. If you do not reach your goals, evaluate what adjustments you can make.
- **Research New Markets:** Once you have established a solid foundation in your primary market, consider expanding into new markets. This may include selling internationally or diversifying into different demographic groups.
- **Seize Opportunities:** Stay alert for growth opportunities, such as trade shows, collaborations, and new distribution channels. These opportunities can be key to your expansion.
- **Sustainability and Responsibility:** As you scale, ensure that you maintain a focus on sustainability and social responsibility. This not only benefits the planet but can also improve your brand's perception among consumers.

Conclusion of Chapter 14

Scalability and growth are ongoing processes that require continuous adaptation and strategic planning. You will be better prepared to face challenges and seize opportunities by reinvesting profits, increasing production in a controlled manner, diversifying your product line, and following a revenue-based expansion plan. With a clear vision and a focus on quality, your clothing brand can reach new heights and establish itself as a significant player in the industry.

Conclusion

Creating a clothing brand is an exciting and challenging journey that requires dedication, effort, and a clear vision. In this conclusion, we'll discuss what you can expect on your path as an entrepreneur, the key lessons you've learned during the process, and helpful tips for staying focused and overcoming obstacles.

Final Thoughts: What to Expect on Your Entrepreneurial Journey

Venturing into the fashion industry is an adventure filled with ups and downs. From the moment you decide to take the first step to the launch of your brand, you will encounter a series of challenges and opportunities.

- **Realistic Expectations:** It's crucial to set realistic expectations. Success does not come overnight. There will be moments of doubt, frustration, and unexpected delays. It's important to be patient and remember that each step, whether small or large, brings you closer to your goal.
- **Adaptability:** The fashion market is dynamic and constantly changing. You must be prepared to adapt to new trends and consumer demands. Flexibility and a willingness to learn will help you survive and thrive.
- **Building Relationships:** Along your journey, you will have the opportunity to build valuable relationships with other entrepreneurs, designers, suppliers, and customers. These connections can open doors and provide support during challenging times.
- **Ethics and Sustainability:** Now more than ever, consumers value sustainability and ethical production. Ensure that your brand reflects these values, as this will not only benefit the environment but also attract a more conscious and loyal audience.

Key Lessons Learned in Creating a Clothing Brand

- **Know Your Market:** Conducting thorough market research is essential. Understanding your target audience, their preferences, and purchasing behaviors will allow you to make informed decisions and design products that truly resonate with them.
- **The Importance of a Clear Vision and Mission:** Having a defined vision and mission will guide all your decisions. This will not only help you stay focused but also attract people who share your values.
- **Prototypes and Testing:** Don't underestimate the importance of creating prototypes and gathering feedback. This will allow you to adjust your products before launching them in the market, which can save you time and resources in the long run.
- **Proper Budgeting:** Solid financial management is crucial for the survival of your brand. Setting a budget and monitoring your expenses will help you identify areas for improvement and ensure that your brand grows sustainably.
- **The Power of Digital Marketing:** Today, digital marketing is a powerful tool for fashion brands. Learning to utilize social media and other digital platforms will help you effectively reach your audience.

Tips for Staying Focused and Overcoming Obstacles

- **Set Short and Long-Term Goals:** Define specific and achievable goals, both short-term and long-term. This will help you stay motivated and focused on your objectives as you progress.
- **Surround Yourself with Support:** Seek mentors, peers, and entrepreneurial communities that can offer you support and advice. Sharing your experiences and learning from others will help you maintain perspective and find solutions to the problems you encounter.
- **Practice Resilience:** Resilience is key to success in any venture. Learn to view failures as opportunities to grow and improve. Each challenge you face can teach you a valuable lesson that will help you in the future.
- **Maintain Your Passion:** Remember why you started this journey in the first place. Keep your passion for fashion alive and your desire to make a difference. This will give you the energy and motivation needed to keep going, even during tough times.
- **Prioritize Self-Care:** The entrepreneurial path can be exhausting. Make sure to take care of yourself, both physically and mentally. Taking breaks, practicing meditation, or engaging in activities you enjoy will help you stay balanced and focused.

Final Reflection

Creating a clothing brand is a journey full of opportunities, insights, and personal growth. You will be on the right path to success if you are prepared to face challenges, learn from experiences, and maintain your passion for fashion. Your brand can not only thrive but also leave a lasting mark on the industry with the right dedication and strategy. Dare to pursue your biggest dreams and create the brand you have always longed for!

Made in United States
Orlando, FL
04 December 2024

54993570R00046